CAREERS IN

STATISTICS

STATISTICIANS USE MATHEMATICAL TECHNIQUES to collect and interpret information. The work is based on numbers, but unlike mathematicians who work on theoretical problems, statisticians use the numbers to solve real-life problems. Statisticians contribute to society in many ways. Some do serious work like finding ways to reduce hunger and disease, or studying the effects of global climate change on food supplies. Others help professional athletes up their game or help political candidates get elected.

The biggest employer of statisticians is the federal government. Government statisticians work in just about every agency. For example, the Department of Labor has a large staff of statisticians studying things like employment rates, wage changes, growing and shrinking job sectors, and the demographic makeup of the workforce. The Department of Agriculture needs to know about crop conditions, livestock inventories, and how crops can be used for new products, and no mission at NASA proceeds without the thumbs up from their staff of statisticians.

There is an obvious need for statisticians across all levels of government, but the demand is even greater outside the public sector. Statistical skills can be used to draw valuable insights from data in just about any industry. In fact, roughly 90 percent of America's industries use statistics in their daily operations. Since the advent of the computer, organizations of all kinds have been collecting and handling huge amounts of data. Computers can crunch the numbers, but statisticians are needed to analyze and interpret the data. They turn data into usable information that non-statisticians can understand and use to make good decisions.

Statistics is the basis of one of the oldest professions in the world. Statistics were used to curb the spread of epidemics in the Middle Ages, and even ancient empires used them to track things like their populations, taxes, and important commodities like cattle. Yet the time has never been better to be a statistician. The career opportunities are so diverse, that statisticians can apply their knowledge to nearly any area they are passionate about. The demand for statisticians is at an all-time high. Employment for statisticians is growing fast, and so are their salaries. The median salary for those with less than three years of experience is $80,000, and that amount can double after being in the profession for at least nine years.

Statisticians are well compensated due to the level of expertise and skill required. Anyone with an aptitude for numbers and critical thinking skills can study statistics in an undergraduate program at a university. A bachelor's degree is enough to qualify for many entry-level jobs, but most professional statisticians go on to earn at least a master's degree in the field, if not a PhD.

Future statisticians can expect excellent earnings, benefits, working conditions, travel opportunities, and job security. It is not surprising that this career is ranked near the top of every list of "best jobs."

WHAT YOU CAN DO NOW

IT TAKES AT LEAST A FOUR-YEAR COLLEGE DEGREE to start a career in statistics. Make sure you know the entrance requirements for the colleges you are considering and work those courses into your high school schedule. The requirements will vary somewhat among different schools, but the focus will always be on math. Take as many advanced math classes as possible. The most important are AP Statistics and AP Calculus.

You will need more than just math classes to be ready for this career. Statistics are meaningless if you cannot interpret data and explain the results to other people. English, debate, and speech classes can help you build important communication skills. Statisticians also play a key role in psychology, and use computers constantly in their daily work. Learn all you can about computers and consider at least one class in psychology. Other helpful classes include social science, current events, and a foreign language.

Learn more about what statisticians actually do. Ask your guidance counselor to arrange a job shadow or invite a statistician to speak on career day. Take advantage of the opportunity to ask for advice. Ask questions and take notes. Find out how they got started and what they like best (or least) about their work. If at all possible, meet several different kinds of statisticians to get an idea of the options that may be open to you. If a particular specialty captures your interest, consider taking some classes that are related to that specialization. You can learn more about statisticians by joining professional associations and attending their local workshops.

Pay attention to the national news. You may be surprised at how many ways statistics are used and how they affect so many different people. Get in the habit of following trends by reading business and trade magazines.

HISTORY OF THE CAREER

BASIC FORMS OF STATISTICS HAVE been used for many centuries. It was common for some early empires to record trade numbers of various commodities. Other ancient states collected details about their populations through a census. The Roman Empire, for example, gathered extensive data on the empire's population, geographical area, and wealth. In the 5th century BC, the Greeks began to apply statistical methods to specific problems. In the book, *History of the Peloponnesian War*, historian Thucydides described how the Athenians calculated the height of ladders necessary to scale the walls of Platea. This information was used to capture this town, which was allied with their enemy Sparta.

The earliest writing on statistics was the 9th century book, *Manuscript on Deciphering Cryptographic Messages*. In it, Muslim philosopher, Al-Kindi, described how to use statistics and frequency analysis to decrypt coded messages. It would be another 500 years until statistics was written about extensively. *The Nuova Cronica*, by Italian banker Giovanni Villani, was the first book to define statistics as a broad-reaching concept. He described statistical information related to population, ordinances, commerce, trade, education, and religious facilities.

Flemish mathematician, Simon Stevin, created the decimal system in 1585. Although the Greeks had long known about the concept known as the arithmetic mean, it was not generalized until the 16th century. That is believed to be the result of the decimal system facilitating the necessary calculations.

In 1662, British demographer John Graunt and economist William Petty, developed census methods that provided the foundation for modern demography. Their greatest achievement was producing the first life table, which indicated the probabilities of survival according to age. Their book, *Natural and Political Observations Made upon the Bills of Mortality*, included mortality rolls of the population in London, which officials used in their attempt to create a system to track the spread of bubonic plague in the city.

The term "statistics" was first used in the mid-18th century. At that time, it was defined as the systematic collection of demographic and economic data by states. That only made sense since the original scope of statistics was intended as a tool for governance, but the definition evolved over time, as statistical methods were applied to the analysis of anything of a scientific or commercial nature. It eventually became defined as the collection of information for anything that required statistical extrapolation.

Several concepts were introduced in the late 1700s that advanced the field of statistics. These included the first timeline charts, the law of probabilities, and graphical representations of statistics. Scottish political economist, William Playfair, originated several types of these visual aids. The line chart, bar chart, histogram, pie chart, and circle graph all proved extremely useful in showing part-whole relationships.

The power of statistics for the public good became evident in England in the mid-1800s when a devastating cholera epidemic ravaged a certain section of London.

Local physician, John Snow, surveyed the city to determine where the disease was active. He then used that data to create a map showing the affected areas and proceeded to interview people within those areas. He was finally able to pinpoint the problem – an infected water supply from a particular pump. The pump was sealed and the cholera epidemic receded. Before Snow's research, it was unknown that cholera could be transmitted through contaminated water. His statistical methods revealed an important fact that has saved countless lives since.

Another hero of the 19th century was Florence Nightingale, who also spearheaded the application of statistical analysis to health problems. Although her methods were somewhat crude by modern standards, she was able to advance epidemiological knowledge and public health practices.

By the late 1800s, probability theory and statistics had become systematized. As a result, statistics moved into new realms outside of governance and public policy. Social scientists used statistical reasoning and probability models to advance the new sciences of experimental psychology and sociology, while physical scientists did the same for thermodynamics and statistical mechanics. Other new concepts, such as standard deviation, correlations, and regression were used to study a wide variety of human characteristics.

Modern statistics became fully developed in the late 19th and early 20th century. At the turn of the century, statistics was transformed into a rigorous mathematical discipline that could be used for analysis, scientific research, and for many types of industrial and political purposes. British statistician and geneticist, Ronald Fisher, wrote two seminal textbooks: *Statistical Methods for Research Workers* and *The Design of Experiments* became the definitive resources for universities around the world. Fisher is also known for being the first to use the statistical term variance, and for applying statistics to evolution.

The field of statistics had exploded by the mid-20th century. Since 1945, the number of universities offering graduate degree programs in statistics has soared from six to more than 100. Even so, the demand for statisticians outpaced the supply as more and more important uses of statistical methods became known. By the time computers were available, the field was more than ready to exploit them.

Computers have provided statisticians with numerous advantages. They allow for more elaborate statistical computation, and facilitate the collection and aggregation of massive amounts of data. A computer can do the work of hundreds of human statisticians, processing millions of records, each with hundreds of separate measurements. Computers can quickly produce simple, accurate summaries based on tens of thousands of permutations that would never be possible by hand.

Today, data is collected and statistically analyzed in every imaginable area of government, business, science, industry, and sports. It has become a common part of our lives and some even use statistics as a hobby. Government officials remain the most dependent on statistics for everything from political races and public health policy to traffic control and military planning - but statistics has gone far beyond governmental needs. The same statistical methods used to analyze blood hormone levels are also used to study waves from distant galaxies, and find concentrations of atmospheric pollutants. Experts predict that the demand for statisticians with expertise in every field of study, from entertainment to nanoscience, will continue to grow as new ways to apply statistical methods are discovered.

WHERE YOU WILL WORK

THERE ARE ROUGHLY 21,000 STATISTICIANS working in the US. They can be found employed in nearly every industry and at all levels of government. The largest employers of statisticians are the federal government, insurance carriers, pharmaceutical and medical device manufacturers, engineering firms, scientific research and development services, healthcare and social service providers, academic institutions, and technical consulting services.

About a third of statisticians work for the government. There are more jobs at the federal level than state and local combined. The federal agencies that hire the most statisticians (also known at the federal level as mathematical statisticians) include the US Census Bureau, Bureau of Economic Analysis, National Agricultural Statistics Service, and Bureau of Labor Statistics. These are just the biggest employers. There are many others, like the National Weather Service and Health and Human Services.

In the private sector, the two biggest employers of statisticians are insurance carriers and pharmaceutical manufacturers. In both cases, they typically work in multi-disciplinary teams made up of various professionals. For example, a pharmaceutical manufacturer that needs to test a new drug for government approval might put together a team that includes statisticians, medical scientists, chemists, pharmacologists, and physicians. Team members working for insurance companies are more likely to include professionals that are closely related. For example, statisticians may work with actuaries to determine the risks of insuring certain situations.

Statisticians typically work in modern well-equipped offices. For some there is occasional travel. Some statisticians may travel to meet face-to-face with team members. Others travel to set up surveys, review and give advice on research projects, or oversee the collection of data. There are also opportunities to travel to attend seminars and conferences, usually at the employer's expense.

Most statisticians, about 80 percent, work full time. Work schedules are usually normal business hours, Monday through Friday. However, deadline rushes and last-minute requests may require overtime.

THE WORK YOU WILL DO

THE AMERICAN STATISTICAL ASSOCIATION defines statistics as "The science of learning from data." In practical terms, statisticians are trained to use data to make decisions. They analyze data and apply statistical techniques to solve real-world problems in business, finance, healthcare, agriculture, public safety, and many other fields.

Every statistical project starts with collecting data. This can be done by designing surveys, taking opinion polls, or conducting studies and experiments. The most common methods, surveys and polls, can be different types and sizes. For example, the national census includes data from nearly everyone living in the US. There are other few projects that require that much data. Most of the time, statisticians use random sampling to collect data from a small number of people in a particular group. After analyzing the data, statisticians interpret the data and explain the results to their clients in a way the client can understand. Some studies take only a few months to complete, while others can take years of work.

Statisticians spend much of their time working on a computer, setting up models, manipulating data, analyzing what they see, and writing reports. Although this work is based on numbers, statisticians should not be mistaken for number crunchers. Their expertise is analyzing and explaining what the numbers mean, and offering advice based on their conclusions. When they are not on the computer, they are in meetings and planning sessions, exchanging ideas with colleagues and reporting their findings to clients.

Unlike most professions, statistics can be applied to just about any field or issue from the environment, to sports and public safety, to entertainment. Employers can therefore come from any organization, public or private, from a small business to the federal government. For example, a retail business will have a database of all its customers, sales activities, orders, and invoices. A statistician can analyze this data to determine customer preferences, peaks and valleys in the sales cycle, failed strategies, and more. They can make recommendations to improve customer satisfaction, add new products that are coming into vogue, remove products that are not producing sufficient profit, change pricing or distribution channels, and increase employee efficiency.

A statistician's skills can be applied to any specific issue, such as inventory control, disease distribution, television viewer demographics, industrial quality control, safety and efficacy of pharmaceuticals, traffic patterns, or projecting demand for new products.

Statisticians do not work in a vacuum. They usually are part of a team, collaborating with professionals in other disciplines. For example, they may work with chemical engineers and medical scientists to determine the effectiveness of new drugs, or they may partner with industrial designers to find ways to improve the aerodynamic characteristics of new vehicles.

Other assignments might include:

- Monitor and predict disease outbreaks

- Measure the toxicity of food additives

- Design, implement, and analyze clinical studies

- Identify and quantify the potential side effects of drugs

- Study traffic patterns and help redesign highway access points

- Collect data to monitor air pollution levels

- Forecast population and economic trends for pension providers

- Project changes in birth rates and assess the number of teachers that will be needed

The Lifecycle of a Statistics Problem

Every statistics project starts with a question or problem to be solved. Statisticians will often meet many times, either in person or on the phone, with clients to make sure they understand exactly what information is wanted. Once that is clear, they decide what data is needed, where to find it, and what method will be used to collect it. They then develop the survey, questionnaire trial, poll, or experiment. They also design reporting forms and write instructions for workers who do the actual data collection and tabulation. Statisticians sometimes collect data themselves, but more often, they supervise others to do the routine work. Data may be collected over the phone, online, through the mail, or extrapolated from some existing database.

After enough data has been collected, statisticians use specialized statistical software to analyze it. Computers allow them to process huge amounts of data for statistical modeling and graphic analysis. During this process, statisticians will calculate averages, identify trends and relationships, and conduct tests to determine the data's reliability and validity. For example, they must account for high non-response rates or sampling errors when drawing conclusions. They need to explain limitations of the data to prevent their clients from making poor decisions based on the results. Statisticians are always trying to find ways to analyze data more accurately and efficiently. Some even help create new software to help them do that.

Presenting results is said to be the most difficult part of this job. Clients, upper level managers, regulatory authorities, and journalists can easily misinterpret the results. Statistics is a science of trends and probabilities, not certainties. Many non-statisticians find it difficult to grasp that concept. Fortunately, statistics is also a visual science. Statisticians can make their point clear by using visual aids such as charts, graphs, tables, and maps. They also write reports, sometimes in two versions: one for team members and another for clients who may not understand the lingo in the first. In some cases, the project may have far-reaching implications. Statisticians may report on those by writing peer-reviewed papers or articles for publication.

Statisticians With Special Expertise

The scope of statistician jobs is far reaching. Statisticians may work in related fields and professions, or in fields that have nothing to do with math or science. This can make for some very interesting choices that suit the individual statistician's personal or professional interests. Through additional training or experience working in a particular area, many statisticians become specialists. Some of the most common specializations include the following.

Healthcare

Statisticians specializing in healthcare are known as biostatisticians or biometricians. They work in pharmaceutical companies, public health agencies, or hospitals. Some design studies to test whether drugs successfully and safely treat medical conditions. Others help identify the sources of outbreaks of diseases in humans and animals. Still others help develop medical devices, evaluate the effects of lifestyle choices on overall health, and study the health effects of aging and environmental factors.

Research and development

Statisticians design experiments for product testing, develop marketing strategies and prices, and analyze consumer trends.

Government statisticians

Most work for the federal government, which is concerned with a large population that is constantly changing. Depending on the agency, a statistician might collect and monitor data like unemployment rates and wages, birth and death rates, the effects of immigration on various sectors, the number of people who have a certain disease, and how demographic distribution is evolving. Some government statisticians have very specific jobs like monitoring the level of pesticides in drinking water or the number of endangered species living in a particular area.

Market research analysts research and analyze market conditions for particular products or services.

They can tell companies what products consumers want, which customers are likely to purchase the company's products, where and what kind of advertising will yield the best results, and what future sales might look like. Their conclusions are based on data collected from consumer surveys, focus groups, or actual sales results. Market research analysts are usually hired to gather this information before a product is developed or launched. Therefore, their work often overlaps that of the research and development team.

Data analysis has been one of the fastest growing areas for statisticians for decades.

In order to successfully compete in the marketplace, businesses of all sizes depend on statisticians to analyze vast amounts of customer and industry data. Large organizations often have a "business intelligence" department that typically includes several statisticians.

Environmental statisticians conduct environmental studies for both government and industry organizations.

The environment is a vast topic and therefore, statisticians working in this sector typically have expertise in many different areas. For example, they may specialize in climatology, assessing changes in climate patterns. In epidemiology, they may evaluate the effects of air pollution on asthma occurrence. Some environmental statisticians assess the potential risks and track the effects of extreme events like floods or nuclear accidents. Others are involved in compliance issues to ensure that legislation protecting our clean air and drinking water is observed.

Sports statisticians

Using a variety of formulas to collect and interpret data, they can help improve team performance, accurately predict outcomes, and help athletes to address their weak spots. They are best known for helping team owners and managers add players to the roster by evaluating potential candidates and determining the best choices. Employers are often surprised by the choices, but the numbers do not care who is the most famous or well liked, only who will work out best for the team.

PROFESSIONALS TELL THEIR OWN STORIES

I Work in the Pharmaceutical Industry

"I always had a strong interest in math subjects in school and both my parents were doctors. In my third year of college, I learned about the work of biostatisticians and determined it was a perfect fit for my combination of aptitude and background. It has turned out to be an interesting and challenging career that I enjoy very much.

I work in clinical development, providing statistical support to clinical studies. Most of the studies are designed to determine the effectiveness and safety of a particular drug. I follow each study from its conception, through all phases of development, to writing the final full clinical study report.

Throughout the process, I closely follow regulatory guidelines.

What I do each day depends on what stage the study is in. I generally spend half the day in front of the computer and the rest in teleconferences and face-to-face meetings. The work of biostatisticians is global in nature, so there are a lot of internet meetings and routine international travel. I like that things are always on the move and that I get to work with so many smart and interesting people. It is certainly never boring.

There has never been a better time to enter this profession. There is great demand for biostatisticians and numerous avenues to pursue. I happen to work for a pharmaceutical manufacturer, but there are opportunities in biotech companies and clinical research organizations. More experienced biostatisticians can find consulting opportunities, working as a contractor rather than as a permanent employee. Consultants are at the top of the pay scale, plus they get to pick and choose the most interesting projects. For all career options, there are possibilities for flexible and remote working.

My advice to future biostatisticians is to establish a network of colleagues that can be a resource throughout your career. It will pay off in many ways, from brainstorming when you're stuck, to looking for a new position."

I Work in Agricultural Statistics

"I am a consultant so I work for both government and private concerns. My expertise is in pesticide use and pesticide residues. Most of what I do is exploratory data analysis (research) and model validation. I love the research because I'm very curious about how the world works and data can help me figure that out, but most of the time I'm doing model validation.

My day varies depending on the project. I spend a lot of time reading documentation of the model I'm supposed to validate. It's actually quite a creative process to figure out what could possibly be wrong. There could be unsubstantiated assumptions, misused data, misinterpreted output, or just plain human error. I will run through the original design process to see if I arrive at the same answer. Regardless if the model is good or not, my job ends with a big report for my client.

There are many misconceptions about statisticians. The main one is it's all about math. I rarely do math. That's what computers are for, but I do need to understand the math. People also think I'm on the computer all day. I actually spend more time in meetings than on the computer. Most would think this work is stuffy. On the contrary, there are plenty of opportunities to be creative. I especially enjoy building tools to display my data and creating publication-quality graphics."

I Work for a Major Gaming Publisher

"Like most companies with online consumers, mine has a huge amount of user behavior data. My routine work deals with market research – monitoring the demographics, checking on quality control, tracking sales, and projecting when a game is in need of an upgrade. That does not usually require any complex analyses. Sometimes I get to go beyond pulling simple data from SQL and work on some text (data) mining or reactive dashboards.

The job prospects are great for statisticians. Anyone with a degree in statistics can certainly find a good opportunity within a month or so into your job search. Once you're in the field, recruiters will start sending invitations to you directly, especially if you have some particularly interesting experience on your résumé. It doesn't have to be years of experience either.

The best advice I can give to those entering the profession is to stretch yourself and get some experience outside of statistical work. Take jobs in industries that interest you even if you won't be doing any statistical work. You've already gotten the education in statistics. Don't be afraid to learn as much as you can about any industries that interest you. That knowledge will make you a more valuable job candidate. Also take advantage of professional development opportunities, like participating in mentoring programs or speaking at conferences."

PERSONAL QUALIFICATIONS

STATISTICIANS OBVIOUSLY NEED outstanding math skills to develop their models and analyses. Agility on the computer is a technical skill that cannot be overrated. Though strong math and technical skills form the foundation of this work, it takes additional personal skills and specific ways of thinking to ensure success as a statistician. There are various ways to describe good statisticians, including the following.

Critical thinkers

Statisticians are faced with complex problems every day. They must be able to work through large amounts of bits and pieces of seemingly unrelated information and arrive at meaningful and accurate conclusions. Critical thinking is the intellectually disciplined process that involves logic and reasoning to form objective judgments.

Clear communicators

Like most professions, there is common jargon used among statisticians. However, statisticians often need to explain their work to people who do not speak "math." They are often called upon to make formal presentations, write reports, propose solutions, and make recommendations to various individuals and groups. They must be able to succinctly and effectively get their points across to a diverse audience.

Quick learners

Statisticians work in nearly every industry and on many different projects within their application area. To solve a problem presented to them, they must first understand the problem and the environment in which it exists. Being able to quickly grasp the fundamentals of a field is enormously helpful. In addition, statisticians need to get up to speed fast in order to determine which technical tools and concepts are most appropriate before starting a new project.

Macro thinkers

Statisticians are often mired in massive data of varying importance. All those details would be distracting and confusing to most people, but successful statisticians are able to size them up in context with the big picture.

Flexible adapters

Statisticians work in a dynamic environment. Changes can occur without warning. Management or clients may come and go, projects may suddenly become urgent or be shut down, or the business climate may shift abruptly. Statisticians should be able to anticipate how their environment might create sudden changes. Successful statisticians enjoy the challenges of constant change, and even thrive on it.

Time jugglers

Statisticians often work on multiple projects simultaneously. For each, there will inevitably be unexpected requests and problems to deal with. This can quickly throw off a carefully planned schedule and lead to a stressful work overload. Experienced statisticians know how to manage time with wiggle room built in to accommodate unanticipated demands. It is impossible to predict what those demands will be, but you can be sure they will occur. Statisticians know how to prioritize tasks based upon their importance, deadlines, and time required to do the work. They are also flexible and ready to reprioritize as the situation changes.

Team players

Statisticians often work in teams. The team, which usually includes professionals from other fields, can change from one project to the next. Strong interpersonal skills are needed to work well with all kinds of people.

Lifelong learners

Statisticians are active learners, always curious about the implications of new information that may affect their future problem solving. The profession is always changing, with new techniques, methods, and software coming along every day. Successful statisticians set aside time every day to keep abreast of new developments.

ATTRACTIVE FEATURES

STATISTICIANS ENJOY ONE OF THE BEST JOBS out there. For the past 10 years, it has been ranked near the top of the list of best careers by numerous publications and surveys. The Wall Street Journal, The New York Times, and The Washington Post have all published encouraging words for those pursuing this career. It has even been referred to as the "hot job" of the decade. A degree in statistics is like the golden ticket to a good and secure job, but it offers much more to excite prospective careerists.

The demand for statisticians is well beyond that of the average occupation, and that demand is growing fast. With a 10-year job growth rate of 30-plus percent, the number of openings is sure to outpace the number of graduates to fill the available positions. That means new statisticians can be assured of a job and even be selective about where they work.

As opportunities expand, so do salaries for these professionals. For the first three years, statisticians earn a median annual salary of about $80,000. That number nearly doubles for those with at least nine years of experience. To get the most return for their investment in education, statisticians could go where the action is. Employers in the hottest industries, like finance and electronics, offer significantly higher pay than insurance carriers and most government agencies. Those high-paying jobs are found in finance and tech centers, like Silicon Valley and New York.

There is much variety in the world of statistics. Because statistics is involved in just about everything, from agriculture to zoology, statisticians can choose to work in nearly any industry or level of government. The skills that form the foundation for statistics can be easily transferred from one field to another. Most statisticians eventually focus on one or maybe a handful of application areas, but even within each area, there is much variety. The range of options is continuously expanding, especially in technical fields like automated tracking, bioinformatics, environmental science, genetics, and nanotechnology.

Successful professionals love what they do and are rarely bored. The work is very creative and intellectually stimulating. Each project is unique, and problems are rarely clear-cut. This leaves plenty of room to be imaginative. The field is also filled with smart and dynamic people. Working with a wide variety of interesting people from different backgrounds and disciplines adds another layer of interest to the work.

The professional rewards are clear, but there are also many personal benefits. There are many ways that statisticians can help make the world a better place. Some protect endangered species while others find the best ways to manage the impacts of climate change. Some combat human rights abuses, and others make medical treatments more effective. Whatever their personal interests or causes, there are ways in which statisticians can have a positive impact.

UNATTRACTIVE ASPECTS

THERE ARE DOWNSIDES ASSOCIATED with every career, but they are hard to find in this field. Statisticians have voiced few complaints and only you can decide if they outweigh the pluses.

Only excellent students who love working with numbers have a chance of success. The educational track is rigorous and it starts in high school. College admissions officers want to see good grades in advanced classes. One of those classes is AP Statistics – reportedly a very challenging and demanding class. Students must see past that first taste of statistics to get to the more interesting college coursework. It turns out the work itself is actually quite different (and arguably more fun) than the AP course describes.

There are plenty of statistician jobs open to those with a bachelor's degree. However, advancement opportunities and pay increases will be limited for those without a graduate degree. This is a diverse field with new options opening up all the time. In many cases, the new opportunities are in technical fields. Getting into new areas like nanotechnology or bioinformatics requires a master's degree at minimum. If the work involves serious research, a PhD will be needed.

Statisticians earn good money, but some say not good enough. Pay varies depending on experience, location, and employer. Experience is highly valued in this field and employers are not willing to give big salary raises to newcomers. You are expected to pay your dues and learn on the job for the first few years. Reaching the six-figure income level is a slow process compared to some other professions. If you want to get there within five years, you need to be in a major city and specialize in a hot area. Unlike many professions, the pay is lowest in academia.

This is a creative field that is open to new thinking. However, only those with at least five years of experience are invited to express new ideas. Assertiveness early in this career is not welcome. You need to have shown solid work at lower levels before pushing new ideas.

Statisticians are not generally recognized for making the essential contributions they do. Their work may well save us all from global climate change, hunger, and disease. But they just do not have the same public image as an astronaut, brain surgeon, or physicist.

EDUCATION

ALL STATISTICIANS NEED A COLLEGE EDUCATION. A bachelor's degree in statistics or mathematics is sufficient to qualify for many entry-level jobs. Those who want to advance beyond low-level work, however, will need at least a master's degree. A PhD is typically required to be considered for a job in academia or to plan and direct research.

Roughly, 100 universities offer graduate degrees in statistics. A typical program naturally leans heavily toward advanced math subjects. Required courses may include linear algebra, calculus, experimental design, survey methodology, probability, and statistical theory. Suggested, but elective coursework includes subjects like logic, psychology, and social science. Because statisticians work daily with data analysis software, computer-programming courses should be considered, even if not required.

While most statisticians have degrees in mathematics, statistics, economics, or another quantitative field, many employers prefer statisticians with a graduate degree in the related discipline of their specialization. Statisticians with a strong background in interdisciplinary fields such as biology or chemistry, for example, will have an advantage when applying for positions in pharmaceutical research and manufacturing. Many colleges and universities also advise statistics students to take courses that will prepare them to work in a variety of industries. The most common choices are computer science, engineering, and physics, but there are numerous other possibilities. Combining statistical skills with just about any other major can provide a distinct competitive advantage when seeking employment.

Continuing education is important for all statisticians. Statistics methods and techniques are constantly changing as they are fine-tuned. Advancing technology also has an effect on nearly every statistician's work. It is important to keep up with what is going on in the world, regardless of whether it is directly related to the statistician's current work. Most statisticians attend conferences or lectures during free time. They are also avid readers.

There are no licensing requirements for statisticians. Membership in professional organizations is also not required. However, many choose to join the ones affiliated with their particular field, such as organizations for economists, manufacturers, or sports management.

EARNINGS

SALARIES FOR STATISTICIANS TYPICALLY START at about $50,000 and go up to more than $130,000 annually. The median annual income works out to roughly $80,000. The most important factor in how much any individual earns is the amount of education and experience that statistician has. The low end of the pay scale is usually populated with entry-level workers and those with only a bachelor's degree. At the high end are professionals with five to ten years of experience and a graduate degree.

A statistician's salary can also vary by industry, type of work, and whether the job is in the public or private sector. The best salaries in the private sector are offered by industries involved in banking and financial services, scientific research, and wholesale marketing of electronics. There are also high-paying jobs in manufacturing, specifically manufacturing of navigational, electromedical, and control instruments. These all generally pay more than $100,000 a year. The lower paying jobs in the private sector are related to insurance activities, healthcare, and social assistance. Private universities are also in this category. These jobs pay about the same as the overall median.

Government agencies tend to pay less than corporations, though there is additional job security and additional benefits to take into account. Statisticians working for agencies at the federal level earn the most, averaging $100,000 a year. State and local government agencies have more budgetary constraints than the federal government, so statisticians are not paid as much. At the low end in the public sector are colleges and universities, which pay about 30 percent less than most federal employers.

Location is another factor that can affect a statistician's salary. Statisticians do best in urban centers where there is a concentration of industries that require the skills of statisticians. The highest statistician salaries can be found in the Silicon Valley (San Jose/Santa Clara, California) area. There the average income is about $140,000. In second place is San Francisco, at $120,000. Keep in mind that salaries are relative. These two places are among the most expensive to live anywhere in the country. A statistician taking that into account might be better off financially by working in Wilmington, Delaware; Raleigh, North Carolina; or Kalamazoo Michigan. The average salaries there are $80,000 to $100,000, but the cost of living is much more affordable.

About 80 percent of statisticians work full time and earn full benefits. Because statisticians are in high demand, signing bonuses and relocation costs are often offered to new recruits.

OPPORTUNITIES

THE JOB OUTLOOK FOR STATISTICIANS is excellent. Employment of statisticians is predicted to grow by more than one third over the coming 10 years. That is much faster than the average for all occupations. There are about 21,000 statisticians working now. Based on these projections, there should be an additional 7,000 new jobs opening up. The job growth will vary somewhat by specific job title and industry. However, the overall demand for statisticians is gaining strength, and this trend shows no signs of slowing.

The use of statistical analysis is more widespread than ever before. The demand for analytical skills is growing in industries like entertainment, advertising, sports, politics, journalism, computer science, and biotechnology. As a result, specialists with a background in areas such as biology, social science, or electronics are in a better position to obtain jobs than general statisticians. In addition, the large increase in available data from the Internet is continuing to open up new areas for analysis.

The need for new treatments and medical technologies has been spurred by the aging of the US. population. As a result, pharmaceutical and medical device manufacturing industries are actively searching for statisticians who can help with scientific research and development. Biostatisticians are particularly sought after. These specialists are needed to conduct the research and clinical trials that are required to obtain approval from the Food and Drug Administration for new products.

Data Science Careers

Big data has had a huge impact on the field of statistics. Big data often involves the collection of data sets that are so vast and intricate, traditional statistical software tools and methodologies are unable to analyze them at a reasonable rate. The result is the emergence of a new interdisciplinary field known as "data science." This is a blend of statistics, computer science, and engineering.

Data scientists are highly educated individuals mostly recruited by academic institutions and independent research firms. They are hired to answer some of the most pressing questions related to epidemiology, environmental health, molecular biology, medicine, biotechnology, bioinformatics, and other technologies.

Government Careers

Job growth in the public sector is related to the general growth in the economy. Statistical analysis is now routinely used to make informed policy decisions. Statisticians with skills in economics are in the best position to land government jobs, but statisticians of every background will find interesting opportunities to make the world a better place. Government agencies, particularly at the federal level, employ large numbers of statisticians for a variety of reasons. Here is a small sampling:

- They study the population and analyze trends in births, deaths, aging, immigration, and education.

- They look at crime patterns and the underlying factors to help policy makers find ways to reduce crime.

- They evaluate our economic relationship to other countries by tracking imports and exports.

- They keep a watchful eye on employment numbers to ensure that the economy is on track.

- They investigate causes and effects of diseases and injuries to determine the most efficient allocation of healthcare and medical research funding.

- They study global climate change and other environmental issues that affect people worldwide.

Honing one's skills is the best way to take advantage of opportunities. An increasing number of jobs in the business sector will require advanced mathematical and statistical knowledge. Candidates with very strong quantitative and data analysis skills will be in a good position to compete for the best job opportunities. Keeping up with new statistical methods is also important to employers. Those with a background in advanced mathematical modeling will find good job opportunities in closely related fields. Employers will also continue to favor prospective employees with computer programming skills. Strong communication skills, which are needed to present data and findings, are very desirable.

Those with only undergraduate degrees will find their opportunities are limited. There will be jobs available, but they will generally be low level, involving minimal responsibility, and performed under rigorous supervision. To get beyond the menial tasks that define low- level jobs in statistics, most statisticians will find it is necessary to obtain a graduate degree.

Advancement opportunities are plentiful for those with substantial experience. Statisticians with at least five years of experience enjoy increased job mobility. They often move from smaller companies to larger ones, or into industries that require more substantial skills and technical expertise. With 10 years of experience, they may move into executive positions or direct research projects.

GETTING STARTED

ONCE YOU HAVE THE SKILLS required for a good job, it is time to go out and find one. Luckily, you are pursuing one of the rare careers where employers compete for good employees (instead of the other way around). Since there are more good jobs for trained statisticians than candidates to fill them, you can afford to be selective and only go after the kind of job you really want. There are a number of ways to locate them, starting with your school.

The career center at your college or graduate school should be your first stop. You will find job postings and notices of career fairs. Ask to be included in emails that announce upcoming visits from recruiters. If you are not on the email list, you could miss out on making a great connection because you did not know about the event.

Some employers skip the recruiters and use internships to screen and recruit future employees. You can find out about internship opportunities at the career center, too. If you find you are in an internship that does not interest you, do not let your disappointment show. The world of statistics is relatively small. Keep up an enthusiastic attitude and you will impress people who can give you good referrals.

You can find job openings for statisticians listed in professional journals and on the websites of professional organizations. If it appears there are not many openings, remember that statistician jobs are usually specialized. Make a list of the many different job titles and search each one. Remember, statisticians are employed by nearly every industry and type of business. Get creative and brainstorm the possibilities.

Work your network. You should have started gathering contacts even before entering college. Contacts can include any professional statisticians you meet, all your teachers and professors, internship supervisors, and alumni from your statistics department that now work in companies that interest you. Keep in touch with these people and let them know you would appreciate hearing about any openings they see coming up.

Make sure you are ready to go when a job you would like opens up. Utilize your career center once again to get help with preparing a polished and honest résumé and cover letter. Use your best English skills – employers will be looking for well-spoken candidates. Do your homework and learn about each company you apply to. Then go the extra mile to tailor your résumé and letter to each.

Develop good telephone interviewing skills. A telephone interview is usually the first step employers use to screen potential employees. The telephone interviewer will probably be an HR person, not a statistician. The interviewer will be checking the basics, such as whether you meet the qualifications and whether you can communicate effectively. Your goal is to get to the next step. You can do that by demonstrating confidence and professionalism, and not present any reason to send your résumé to the pile of rejects.

The next, and most important, step is the face-to-face interview. You can expect to be interviewed by several people, including potential supervisors and coworkers. These will be technical folks, not from HR, who will want to evaluate how you will fit into their team, project, department, and/or company culture. Again, the career center is where you can get help with honing your interviewing skills.

ASSOCIATIONS

■ **American Statistical Association**
www.amstat.org

■ **This is Statistics**
http://thisisstatistics.org

■ **Mathematical Association of America**
https://www.maa.org

■ **Institute of Mathematical Statistics**
http://imstat.org/en/index.html

PERIODICALS

■ **Journal of the American Statistical Association**
https://amstat.tandfonline.com/loi/uasa20

■ **Journal of Statistical Software**
https://www.jstatsoft.org

WEBSITE

■ **National Agricultural Statistics Service**
https://www.nass.usda.gov